'UMAR BIN 'ABD AL-'AZIZ

Yasien Moh

GW00724748

Published by

Ta-Ha Publishers Ltd.
1, Wynne Road
London SW9 0BB

Published by

Ta-Ha Publishers Ltd.
1 Wynne Road
London SW9 0BB

British Library Cataloguing in Publication Data
Mohamed, Yasien
'Umar Bin 'Abd Al-'Aziz
I. Title

ISBN 1-897940-14-9

Typeset by JL & GA Wheatley Design, Aldershot. Tel: (0252) 21298

Printed By: DELUXE PRINTERS Tel: 081-965 1771

INTRODUCTION

'Umar bin 'Abd-al 'Aziz, al Khalifat as-Salih (the pious Caliph), was the eighth of the Umayyad Caliphs. The establishment of the Umayyad Caliphate in Damascus brought an end to the Khalifat-ur-Rashidin (the Caliphate of the Rightly-Guided). The Caliphs who ruled from Madinah followed the example of the Prophet (SAW), seeking no worldly advantage or personal gain. Their sole aim was to implement the law (hukm) of God, as embodied in the Shari'ah.

The word Caliph means "vicegerent" and as the title suggests, the Caliph is not a sovereign ruler having supreme power but is a representative of God, who alone is sovereign. The Rashidin Caliphs attempted to rule with uprightness, justice and compassion. Their personal life-style was abstention (zuhd) and contentment (shukr) with the basic necessities of life.

By contrast, the rule of the Umayyads was characterised by worldliness. For the most part, these Caliphs were motivated by the quest for wealth and power, leading lives of extravagance, and selfish indulgence amidst much pomp and ceremony. 'Umar bin 'Abd-al Aziz was the shining exception. He stood out like a beacon amongst all the Umayyads, worthy of being compared to the Rashidin Caliphs in character and in authority. Thus, he was considered the fifth of the Rashidin Caliphs, despite being the eighth in line of the Umayyad dynasty.

Like the Rashidin Caliphs, he saw his rule as a divine

1

service, dutifully recognising the full extent of his responsibility. On one occasion he wept when he realised the awful extent of his responsibility and his accountability to God. His disregard for personal gain was illustrated by his giving all his personal wealth to the Bayt-al-Mal (Public Treasury), requesting his wife to do the same. It is for all these reasons that his rule is regarded as part of the Khalifat-al-Kamila (The Perfect Caliphate) of the Rashidin Caliphs.

'Umar bin 'Abd-al-Aziz was widely celebrated for his just rule. Muslims as well as non-Muslims throughout the vast Islamic empire were content except for the Umayyad royal family. They were no longer able to live extravagantly and behave ostentatiously. Thus, in their attempt to remove 'Umar bin 'Abd-al-Aziz from the throne, they poisoned him. In 101 AH, two years and five months after ascending to the Caliphate he died.

Umar was a descendant of Umar bin-al Khattab (RA); his mother being the daughter of the pious girl in this story.

Dr. Yasien Mohamed

'UMAR BIN 'ABD AL-'AZIZ

In the late hours of the night, al-Faruq 'Umar bin-al Khattab (may God be pleased with him!) used to wander through the lanes of the city to survey the condition of the community (Ummah) since he had become Caliph.

On one such occasion, while passing a few houses just before dawn, he was struck by the argument of a pious girl. He stopped to listen.

"My dear daughter," the mother said, "get up and pour some water into the milk so there will be more to sell." The young girl replied, "But the Commander of the Faithful, 'Umar bin-al-Khattab, has forbidden us to mix milk with water."
The mother answered: "But where is Caliph 'Umar, he's not watching us now. Now go and mix the milk with some water!"

"Mother," the pious girl replied, "even if 'Umar is not here, God, the Lord of the Universe is always Present."

'Umar (RA) was impressed by her character, piety and godliness. He rushed home to speak to his sons. "I saw a pious girl. Who would like to marry her?" "I already have a wife," said Abdullah. "So have I," added Abdurahman. Asim then said: "I will marry her, father, for I am single and I am happy with your choice."

Asim bin-al-Khattab married her (may God be pleased with them!). They lived happily and were blessed with

3

many children. One of his daughters married 'Abd-al-Aziz bin Marwan, and they were blessed with 'Umar bin 'Abd al-Aziz. Considering his roots, it is not surprising that 'Umar bin 'Abd al-'Aziz turned out to be known for his piety, generosity and justice. The pleasures and profanities of worldly life did not divert him from his attention to the Hereafter.

He was so bent upon establishing justice that neither his critics nor those who envied him could sway him from his purpose. Furthermore, he became a symbol of peace and security to every citizen. He was also eloquent, clear-headed, learned and full of wisdom.

Such were the qualities of 'Umar bin-'Abd-al'Aziz bin-Marwan. His mother, the daughter of Asim bin-'Umar bin-al-Khattab bin-Nufayl, was from the family of Adi bin-Kan. She too, was like her mother — gentle, pleasant and God-fearing. Thus, 'Umar acquired noble qualities from both sides of his family and was called Abu-Hafs.

Birth

'Abd-al-'Aziz bin-Marwan, the father of 'Umar bin-'Abd-al-Aziz, transferred the administration of his governorship in Egypt to the city of Hulwan, where he was blessed with a son, 'Umar, in the sixty-third year of the Hirjrah. His parents were overjoyed by his birth.

Upbringing

'Abd-al-'Aziz bin-Marwan was determined to rear his son Islamically. He made sure 'Umar memorised the Qur'an

4

while young, later sending him to Madinah in pursuit of further knowledge. Madinah was an ideal centre for learning because some Companions of the Prophet (SAW), were still present at his Mosque. In this blessed environment 'Umar (May God be pleased with him!) received his early training in Islamic jurisprudence, Prophetic traditions, and poetry. Through his personal initiative and determination to learn he developed an incorruptible mind with a capacity for sound judgement.

A Cherished Desire

Every person has a wish he hopes to fulfill one day. As he grows older, he hopes that through longevity he may realise his wish. 'Umar bin-al-Khattab, who was concerned with the future of the Islamic community (Ummah), said: "I wish one of my sons will fill the world with as much justice as it is filled with oppression."

According to Abdulah bin-Dinar, ibn-'Umar said: "The problems of oppression will never cease until a man from the sons of 'Umar succeeds in the governship of this *Ummah*. That man will have a birthmark on his face."

Marriage

The star, 'Umar bin-'Abd-al-'Aziz, started to shine in the skies of the Islamic community as he began to manifest the signs of his intelligence. He was so handsome and brilliant that all eyes were focused on him when he walked and the learned hung onto his words.

'Abd-al-Malik bin-Marwan was thinking of a husband

for his daughter, Fatimah. He found 'Umar bin-'Abd-al-'Aziz to be a perfect match, and invited him over to Damascus. 'Umar married Fatimah. It was a noble and blessed marriage.

Governor of Madinah

As a student in Madinah, 'Umar pursued his studies in sciences, law and literature. The people of Madinah fondly remembered him as governor of their city, a position delegated to him by al-Walid bin-Abd-al-Malik. Thus, 'Umar had responsibility from an early age. He was only twenty-five years old when he had assumed the governorship of the Prophet's City.

He was always eager to follow the life-style of the Prophet (SAW). He was meticulous about the manner of his *Umrah* and *Hajj* (the Lesser and the Greater Pilgrimage). He was also concerned about perfecting his prayers, his recitation of the Qur'an and sought constant guidance.

Anas bin-Malik (may God be pleased with him!) says: "I never performed prayer behind anyone who had such a great resemblance to the Prophet's prayer (may God accept his prayers and grant him peace!) as this young boy, 'Umar bin-'Abd-al-'Aziz.

'Umar continued as governor for several years, during which time he proved to be a ruler of justice and integrity. In the presence of the Prophet (SAW), the Muslims had experienced the Divine Breeze of justice and mercy blowing towards them. They had been touched by his

goodness, had felt a spiritual intimacy in his company, and had been honoured by his visits. 'Umar bin 'Abd al-'Aziz attempted to follow piety, purity and guidance of the above Prophetic way. His governorship in Madinah, proved to be a fitting prelude to his position as Caliph.

'Umar bin-'Abd-al-'Aziz not only extended the Mosque of God's Messenger while he was governor of Madinah, but also improved and beautified the city. Consequently, the graves of the Prophet (SAW) and his Companions, Abu-Bakr and 'Umar (may God be pleased with them!), came to be incorporated inside the Mosque as we know it today.

He was the best of men to accompany, and the simplest in life-style. When faced with any problem, he used to gather the legal scholars (fuqaha') of Madinah and select ten from amongst them. He never decided on any matter without consulting them. Those who attended his meetings were: Urwa, 'Ubaydullah bin-Utba, Abu-Bakr bin-Abdurrahman bin-al-Harith bin-Hisham, Abu-Baker Sulayman bin-Khathama, Sulayman bin-Yasar, al-Qasim bin-Muhammad bin-Hazm, Salim bin-Ubaydullah, Abdullah bin-Amir bin-Rabi'a, Kharij bin-Zayd bin Thabit, and Said bin-al-Musayyib.

'Umar never deviated from Said bin-al-Musayyib's advice, the jurist (faqih) of the Close Disciples (at-Tabi un). Ibn Musayyib had not bothered to approach the previous Caliphs, until 'Umar bin-'Abd-al-'Aziz became Caliph. Ibn-Musayyib went to him because of his sense of justice and because of his respect for scholars. (Ulama).

Sucession to the Caliphate

Raja bin-Hayawa narrated:

"One Friday, in preparation for Congregational Prayer
(Jumu'ah), Sulayman bin-'Abd-al-Malik put on a green silk
garment. Facing the mirror, he exclaimed: "By God, I am
indeed a young king!"

Sulayman went to prayer with the Friday congregation.
On his return he suddenly had a severe fever. When his
fever worsened, he consulted me concerning the Caliphate. I said: "The Caliph will be protected from punishment
in the grave if he chooses a pious successor."

Sulayman said: "What is your opinion of David, the son
of Solomon?" I said; "He is in Constantinople (Istanbul)."
He said: "Whom would you suggest then?" "Your nom-
ination is the one that counts, Oh Caliph, I shall only give
my opinion regarding the ones you mention," I said. He
asked: "What is your opinion of 'Umar bin-'Abd-al-'Aziz?"
"By God!" I exclaimed, "I know him to be an eminent and
virtuous Muslim."

He agreed: "He certainly is so. But if I were to name him
as my successor to the Caliphate, and leave 'Abd-al-Malik's
sons entirely out of consideration, there will surely be an
upheaval. They will never let him rule over them, unless
I nominate one of them to succeed him. I therefore nominate Yazid ibn-Malik as heir apparent to 'Umar. That will
pacify them." Rajah agreed and wrote: "In the name of
God, the Beneficient, the Merciful! This is a letter from
'Abdullah Sulayman bin-'Abd al-Malik, Commander of the

8

Faithful, to 'Umar bin-'Abd-al'Aziz: "I hereby nominate 'Umar bin-'Abd-al-'Aziz as my successor to the Caliphate, and Yazid bin-'Abd-al Malik as his successor. Listen carefully and obey the new Caliph! Fear God, and do not be divided amongst yourselves, because that will lead to your downfall."

He instructed the chief of police to assemble the royal family. Sulayman told Rajah: "Read my letter and command them to pay homage to 'Umar bin-'Abd-al'Aziz, my successor in the Caliphate." Rajah conveyed the Caliph's orders and they said: "We hear, and we obey."

When they had all left, 'Umar bin-'Abd-al-'Aziz said to me: "O Abu-'al-Miqdam, Sulayman has displayed love, respect, kindness and affection towards me. I fear he has placed too much confidence in me regarding the Caliphate. Therefore, I implore God to relieve me of this heavy responsibility immediately. If not, I may be unable to resign later. Rajah said: "No, by God! I cannot consider your wishes at all. 'Umar left depressed. Rajah reported: "I came to Sulayman bin-'Abd-al-Malik and he was near death. I tried to turn him in the direction of the *Qiblah* (towards Mecca), while he was dying." "Death has not come," he whispered softly. He began to speak, trying to find his last breath. I made two more attempts to turn his face towards the *Qiblah*, but he turned his face away, and after a third attempt, he told me:

"Since you want me to say it, Rajah, I shall say it now: I bear witness that there is no deity except Allah, and I bear witness that Muhammad is His servant and Messenger." Rajah continued: "I laid him on his back, and then he passed away. I closed his eyes, covered him with a green winding sheet, and shut the door: "The Caliph is dead!".

"I charged a responsible person to guard the door, and not to allow anyone to enter without permission. I summoned the royal family, read the letter, and requested the allegiance of the people. They pledged allegiance to 'Umar, and I knew I had fulfilled the Caliph's last request.

"I told them: Stand up; your brother Sulayman has just passed away! They all stood up and responded in the traditional way: 'Verily from God we come, and unto Him do we return!' I took 'Umar by the hand and seated him on the pulpit. The others were still standing, shocked, by the news of Sulayman's death."

Rajah continued: "Sulayman had been cleansed, washed and wrapped in white sheets, while 'Umar bin-'Abd-al-'Aziz prayed for him. When his burial ceremony (*Janazah*) was complete, the Caliphate's transport was brought to him. This comprised of donkeys, horses and mule drivers."

'Umar asked: "What is this for?" They said: "This is for your transportation." "I do not need it. My mule is sufficient for me," commented 'Umar. 'Umar was content with his she-mule. The rest of the horses and donkeys were sold, and the money derived from their sale was given to the Public Treasury (*Bayt-al-Mal*).

After leaving the graveyard, he mounted upon his usual animal and arrived at the Caliphate buildings and was told to dismount there. 'Umar refused, saying: "Abu-Ayyub's wife and family are living here. Do not eject them from their home, my house is sufficient for my needs.

'Umar stayed in his own home until they were able to leave and vacate the place in their own time. Evening arrived, and 'Umar called: "Rajah, please bring me a secretary."

"I called for a scribe, and was impressed by 'Umar's letter which was characterised by eloquence, precision and brevity. He ordered copies to be drawn up, and sent to every major town."

The First Sermon (Khutbah)

'Umar bin-'Abd-al-'Aziz ascended the pulpit, praised God and said:

"Verily there is no Prophet after Muhammad (may God accept his prayers and grant him peace!), nor any revealed Book after the Qur'an.

Whatever God has ordained to be pure is permissible until the Day of Judgement, and whatever God has forbidden, is forbidden until the Day of Judgement. I am no judge to make my own decisions but an executor of God's law. I am no innovator who makes his own laws, but merely an obedient servant who follows God's guidance.

Creation is not designed to disobey the Creator; nor was man made to disobey his Lord. Verily, I am not the best man among you, but merely one man from among you; but, God has burdened me with this great responsibility."

Having expressed his wishes, he stepped down. Thus 'Umar bin-'Abd-al-Aziz became Caliph of all the Muslims. He was a just, and righteous Caliph. People wished his reign would be a long one. His Caliphate marked the last in the line of the Righteous Caliphs (al-Khulafah ar-Rashidin).

But this fifth Rightly-Guided Caliph had no desire for the rank of Caliph because he felt it was a heavy burden and a great responsibility. He did not think of his authority in terms of prestige and status. Nor was he attracted by the pomp and luxury it afforded. This story has already recorded how 'Umar bin-'Abd-al'Aziz returned the horses and mules to the Public Treasury.

'Umar's wife, Fatimah, the daughter of Abd-al-Malik, had some rare jewellery in her possession, the like of which had never been seen before. This had been given to her by her father. It is recorded that he told his wife, Fatimah: "Choose between two alternatives: either return your jewellery to the Bayt-al-Mal or permit me to leave you, for I hate to see those ornaments kept by you now that I am Caliph."

"I'll choose you many times over the jewellery," she responded. Thus, it was taken away and placed in the Public Treasury. Does this not show the nobility of 'Umar's wife and the profound effect he had on her. They were both averse to the comforts of worldly life and its temporary vanities.

Peculiarities and Attributes

'Umar bin-'Abd-al-'Aziz (may God be pleased with him!)

had praise-worthy characteristics and noble attributes. He was elevated by the purity of his soul and exalted in both his private and public life.

When he succeeded to the Caliphate, neither pride, haughtiness or arrogance (that are normally found in a ruler) entered his heart. Instead, he wished to rid himself of these vices, and was willing to step down from the heavy burdens of the Caliphate. It is our great pleasure to describe briefly some of the noble qualities of 'Umar bin-'Abd-al-'Aziz.

Umar's Sense of Justice

Justice was the chief characteristic of the great Caliph, 'Umar bin-'Abd-al'Aziz (May God be pleased with him!). Each situation reveals that his sense of justice stands out clearly above all his other qualities. Even historians affirm that his period was a continuation of the period of the four Rightly-Guided Caliphs, Abu-Bakr, 'Umar 1, 'Uthman and 'Ali (may God be pleased with all of them!).

Muhammad bin-Fudhalah relates that 'Umar bin-'Abd-al-'Aziz passed by the dwelling of a monk from Mesopotamia. This monk had lived a long life, and was known to be learned in the Scriptures. He was from the *Ahl al-Kitab* or "People of the Book". That is, the people from the Jewish and Christian Scriptures. The monk remarked: "Umar is an Imam who has brought justice and guidance." The monk's opinion was highly valued. This shows the extent to which 'Umar-bin-'Abd-al-'Aziz enjoyed respect, love and appreciation. The effect of his justice became widespread until his fame reached as far as Khurasan (north-eastern Persia and western Afghanistan) where he was spoken of by everybody.

Walid bin-Muslim, a man from Khurasan, narrated the following incident: "When a man with a scar from the sons of Marwan rules, swear allegiance to him for he will be a just Imam. Thus, every time a new Caliph came, I asked about him until 'Umar bin-'Abd-al-'Aziz succeeded to the Caliphate. He appeared three times in my dream.

"I went to Damascus, where I met him, and told him what had happened. He asked: What is your name? Where are you from? Where is your home? In Khurasan, I replied. Then I pledged loyalty to him."

This man came all the way from Khurasan. He endured the hardships of travelling merely to pledge allegiance to a just Caliph, willingly without any motivation for reward! The people all knew the obvious difference between 'Umar's rule and that of the previous Umayyad Caliphs.

Wahab bin-Mun'iah once said: "If a *Mahdi* were to arise in this community, it would be 'Umar bin-'Abd-al 'Aziz (May God be pleased with him!). To be sure he ruled with justice, showed concern for his people who had become much more inclined to worship God.

He caused peace (*sakina*) and contentment (*shukr*) to prevail among them. History tells us: "The wolves used to graze alongside the sheep." The people used to ask one another: "Which part of the Qur'an did you read last night?"; "How much charity have you given lately?"

"Have you taken part in any Jihad or Struggle in God's cause?" And, "What do you know about Muslims?"

Just after he succeeded to the Caliphate his wife entered his room. 'Umar was praying with tears streaming down his beard. She said: "O Commander of the Faithful, what's wrong? Why are you weeping?" He replied: "O Fatimah, I have been invested with authority over the Muslim community, both the Arabs and the non-Arabs. I have a heavy responsibility. I was thinking of the poor who are starving, the sick who are destitute, the naked who are in distress, the oppressed who are stricken, the strangers in prison, and the aged. Furthermore I thought of large families with meagre means, living in distant provinces all over the world. I felt that God would make me account-able for them on the Day of Judgement. I feared that no defence on my part could avail me, so I wept."

'Umar was determined to attend to the needs and petitions of people because of his enthusiasm for justice and his accountability to God. When he returned from the funeral of the previous Caliph, and after people has sworn allegiance to him, he was very anxious.

His deputy asked him: "Why are you so worried? This is no time for such an attitude!" 'Umar replied: "Why should I not be sad? Every person in the East or West demands his due from me. I am responsible for his needs, whether he demands his rights in writing or not."

This was his sense of accountability and his determin-ation to act justly towards all his subjects in every respect. 'Umar bin-'Abd-al-'Aziz would never pass judgement

without the advice of his subjects and his learned assoc-
iates. It is said that when he succeeded to the Caliphate,
he called upon Muhammad, Rajah and Salim who were
Learned advisors saying: "I am faced with the burden of
responsibility, please give me advice."

Muhammad bin-Lab advised: "Treat the elderly as your
father, the younger as your brother, and the small child
as your own son. Act righteously towards your father,
mend your relationhip with your brother and be kind to
your son.

Rajah bin-Haywa said: "Please people with what pleases
you, and dislike for others what you dislike for yourself."

And Salim bin-'Abdullah advised him: "Refrain from
the desires of this world, and think of your latest meal as
your last meal before death."

So 'Umar said: "There is no power and no strength
except in God, the Most High!" 'Umar applied justice to
himself before expecting it from his subjects. Once he
gathered all the leaders of the people together and addres-
sed them as follows: "The area called 'Fandak' which
constitutes a village like any other village in Khaybar, was
in the hands of Muhammad (may God accept his prayers
and grant him peace!). Then Abu-Bakr and Umar bin-al-
Khattab assumed this responsibility and used it for the
benefit of all Muslims as it was in the time of the Prophet
(may God accept his prayers and grant him peace!).

"Marwan then divided the land up. I obtained a portion
of it while al-Walid and Sulayman donated their portions

to me. There is nothing worthier than the income I receive from this piece of land. I prefer to give it to the *Bayt al-Mal* as God's Messenger had done."

People has become desperate in the face of the Umayyad's injustice. 'Umar ordered the Umayyads' wealth to be sent to the Public Treasury. This property was called "booty due to injustice" and he returned any illegal wealth to those to whom it rightly belonged.

He told them: "Leave me alone! If not, I shall go to Makkah and resign from the Caliphate for someone more deserving. If I were to live for fifty years among you, it would only be for the purpose of establishing justice." (The Ulama agreed without exception that 'Umar was a just Imam and the Fifth of the Righteous Caliphs).

'Umar bin-'Abd-al-'Aziz worked very hard during the period of his rule. He suppressed all types of injustice and gave every deserving person his due. His town crier used to call out every day: "Where are the creditors? Where are the poor? Where are the orphans?" This call continued until everyone was self-sufficient.

'Umar bin-'Abd-al-'Aziz explained the constitution to the people as follows: "O people, anyone who joins us must agree with us in five matters, or else keep away from us: Bring our attention to those who are unable to express their needs, help us achieve goodness and guide us wherever we are unable to give guidance, do not gossip about anyone during his absence; and do not interfere in matters which do not concern us." Poets and orators avoided him. Legal scholars and pious men stood by him and said: "It is not right for us to abandon this man unless his actions contradict whatever he says. How fine is his constitution, and how clear are his orders!"

Such was 'Umar bin-'Abd-al-'Aziz, a man not intoxicated by his succession to the Caliphate, nor dazzled by its pomp and ceremony. He tried his utmost to act responsibly and worked so hard towards fulfilling other people's happiness, that he had no time to consider his own needs.

His Standing Among Scholars

'Umar bin-'Abd-al-'Aziz had a special place in the hearts of the 'Uluma (scholars) and the fuqaha (law-givers) because of his zeal for acquiring knowledge. His house was a source of knowledge for students, a place of refuge for the 'Ulama, and a sweet spring for those who studied Hadith or Prophetic Traditions.

Abu-Nadhir bin-al-Madya said: "I once saw Sulayman bin-Yasar standing outside the house of 'Umar bin-'Abd-al-'Aziz, so I asked him: "Have you come from 'Umar's home?" "Yes," he said. I said: "Did you teach him anything?" "Yes," he said. "By God," I remarked, "he is more knowledgeable than any of you!" To be sure, 'Umar was a great scholar. Mujahid declared: "We came to Umar to teach him, but we found ourselves learning more from him. He was so widely reputed for his knowledge that it is said of him: "The scholars themselves have become his pupils."

The depth of his understanding of Islamic sciences and

his search for truth and certainty, reached such an extent that al-Layt said: "A man who accompanied Ibn-Umar and Ibn-Abbas told me 'Umar bin-'Abd-al-'Aziz offered him a post: "Whenever we gathered information on a subject, we realised that 'Umar was the most knowledgeable man in the principles and application of every science."

History records many situations which suggest his range of knowledge. Abdullah bin-Tawus said: "I saw my father and 'Umar bin-'Abd-al-'Aziz standing up from evening prayer right up till the daybreak prayer.

When they were finished, I asked my father: "O father, who is this man?" "This is 'Umar bin-'Abd-al-'Aziz; he is one of the righteous reformers of this nation." Such was 'Umar, the narrator of Traditions, pious muhadith (narrator of traditions) and faqih (law-giver). He filled horizons with his knowledge, and became the talk amongst scholars, and a personal source of reference for the fuqaha.

'Umar the Ascetic

'Umar bin-'Abd-al-'Aziz (may God be pleased with him!) was raised in the house of his father, 'Abd-al-'Aziz bin-Marwan. He had a special education, combined with a luxurious upbringing and was exposed to the height of ease and comfort. He used to wear a garment worth four hundred dirhams, and even remarked: "How coarse is this garment!"

But when 'Umar bin-'Abd-al-'Aziz assumed the Caliphate, he refrained from the luxuries of life. He used to wear a garment worth fourteen dirhams only, and considered this as being too expensive. His biography records that 'Umar once came to his wife, and said: "O Fatimah give me a dirham to buy some grapes." He was told that a dirham was not enough; so 'Umar said: "Indeed, this is easier for us than to free ourselves from the chains of Hell tomorrow."

The wealth of the Muslim empire lay at his feet. He could squander it without anyone questioning him about it. But he would not do so, for he was mindful of God, the Most High.

As a result, God kept his hand away from other people's wealth and protected him from it. 'Umar forced himself to live on the bare minimum for his survival. Malik bin-Dinar says: "People say Malik bin-Dinar is an ascetic. But the true ascetic is 'Umar bin-'Abd-al-'Aziz "Even though all the world (dunya) had been given to him, he keeps his hands away from it.

'Umar's Even Temper

'Umar bin-'Abd-al-'Aziz became famous for the forbearance and self-control he manifested in many situations. One night 'Umar entered a mosque. It was dark inside and a guard was standing behind him. While walking in the mosque, he stumbled over a sleeping man. The man raised his voice and shouted in 'Umar's face: "Are you crazy?" 'Umar replied: "No." The guard wanted to attack the man, but 'Umar prevented him saying: "He only asked me if I were crazy, so I told him that I was not." This quality of forbearance which teaches us to suppress our anger, and to forgive in the face of a superior power.

'Umar's son went out to play with some other boys, and one of them injured him. When the boy's mother, Fatimah, heard of this, she screamed and became frantic. When 'Umar enquired about what had happened, the boy's mother, a poor, old woman, approached 'Umar and apologised for what her son had done. She pleaded: "After all, he is only an orphan."

'Umar asked her whether she received money from the Public Treasury. He gave instructions that the boy be listed among those deserving of money from the Public Treasury. Fatimah was angry: "He hit your son, and you give him money!" 'Umar responded: "He is only an orphan and you have frightened him".

A man approached 'Umar, raising his voice. 'Umar merely said: "Do you want the devil to fill me with anger. Do you want me to lose the reward of self-control in the Hereafter when we all meet before the throne of God Almighty?"

Thus 'Umar turned away from him and overlooked the matter. How gentle and forgiving you are, 'Umar! Even though you had the power to destroy, you were gentle to those who spoke foolishly to you. God describes the servants of the Merciful as follows: "They are those who walk around the earth gently, and if some ignorant person addresses them, they say: 'Peace!'" (Q: 25:63).

'Umar's Humility

One night 'Umar had a guest. The lamp in the house went out, and the guest wanted to repair it, but 'Umar did not allow him to do so. He got up himself to repair the lamp. Then said: "I have stood up, and I am 'Umar; I sat down, and I am still 'Umar!" The messenger of God has said: "Anyone who is humble before God will be exalted, and anyone who glorifies Him, is protected by Him."

His Refusal to Accept Presents

A man offered 'Umar bin-'Abd-al-'Aziz an apple as a gift, and said: "O Commander of the Faithful, God's messenger used to accept presents." "Indeed, any gift offered the Prophet was really a free gift; but as far as we are concerned, it means bribery," he replied. This answer exemplifies the poet's saying many times over:

> "Strip yourselves of worldly things
> For naked is how you were born."

Guidelines to Piety and Virtue

'Umar used to advise his companions and fellow administrators in every possible field. He wrote stating: "If the power you have allows you to oppress any people, then remember that the power of God Almighty always stands over you."

He wrote to Addy bin-Addy, saying: "Verily, Islam offers us the Prophet's tradition (*Sunnah*), and a Muslim's compulsory duties (*fard*), and the *Shari'ah* (Islamic code of laws). Anyone who fulfils them completes his faith (*Iman*); but anyone who does not, does not fulfil his faith. As long as I live, I shall explain this to you so that you may act upon it; but if I die, I will not be anxious to live in your company, but in the company of God."

He wrote to some of his administrators: "To heed God (taqwah) is your duty. God does not accept anything besides that. He is Merciful only to those who possess it, and His reward will be only for this quality."

He used to say: "The most loved qualities in God's sight are sincere intention and forgiveness. They become a source of strength, as well as of kindness in ruling."

"If a person is kind and compassionate to his fellow men in this world, God will be most Kind and Compassionate to him on Judgement Day."

Speech on Death

'Umar used to follow the funeral procession (Janazah) of any person. Everyone would disperse except for 'Umar and his companions standing a distance away from the grave-side. His companions asked him: "O Commander of the Faithful, you were a friend of the deceased, yet you have moved away from him as if to leave him alone?" He said: "Yes, is our life in this world not fleeting? Dear ones are lonely and despicable, and rich ones become poor; the youth become senile and decrepit, and the living must die some day. Do not be dazzled by its outward beauty when you know its transcience. The person who is easily deceived is the one who is dazzled by it."

"Where are the citizens who have built its cities, opened up its rivers, and planted its trees? They settled down in it for only a few days. They were deceived by their own good health, and strength. Did they commit any sins? Indeed they were overjoyed by wealth of this world and envious of anyone who accumulated it. What has dust done to their bodies, and what did fire do to their corpses? What will the worms do to their bones and limbs?"

'Umar bin-'Abd-al-'Aziz wrote to some members of his family: "If you sense that death may come to you at night or by day, every transient thing will become hateful to you, and you will begin to love everything that is peaceful and enduring."

'Umar bin-'Abd-al'Aziz gave a speech one day in which he said: "O people, be true to your secrets, and whatever you declare will be sound; work for the Hereafter and your world will become sufficient to you. May peace and blessings of God Almighty rest on you!"

'Umar's Last Words

'Umar said in his last speech: "The spoils of the dead rest in your hands. Those who are still living will leave the spoils in just the same way as others have left them in the past. "Do you not see that each day and night, people keep coming and going? They are being placed in the earth to return to their Lord."

"The crevice is hidden, unlevelled and not smoothed over. You have left your spoils, my dear ones, and are forced to live in the dust, facing your reckoning with God on Judgement Day — poor is he compared with what lies in front of him; rich is he compared with what he has left behind!" By God, I am telling you this because I know that none amongst you knows this, the way that I know it myself." Then he stepped down and did not leave until he was carried away to his final resting place. He left behind him thirteen sons and two daughters.

His Manner of Death

The time for 'Umar to meet his Lord arrived on the 20th day of Rajab in the year 101 AH. He died at the age of 39, after having reigned as Caliph for two years and five months. Fatimah, the daughter of 'Abd-al-Malik and wife of 'Umar bin-'Abd-al-'Aziz, said: "Umar recited the following verses frequently. In his death throes:

"Life in the Hereafter is meant for those who do not choose grandeur and corruption in this world, and success is destined only for the godfearing."

May God's Mercy be with you, just Caliph! May God be pleased with you, Oh Pious Ruler! You have given us a sublime example in your behaviour to every ruler, to every learned man, to every pious follower, to every worshipper, be he rich or poor. Peace be upon you, and upon those who have ruled in righteousness before you, and upon those who follow your example after you!

True Stories
For Children